AFLOAT

Winner of The Birdy Poetry Prize—2025
by Meadowlark Press

Praise for *Afloat*

The punch of certain lines concusses long after you've closed *Afloat*: "From a darkness known only to her / into a light both of us could see." The author explores the many facets, triumphs, illusions, delusions, highs, and lows of being mother, daughter, sister, lover, teacher, creator, nurturer, icon, and rebel. In forceful narrative poems part memoir, lyric, ode, elegy, [and] manifesto, a vibrant musicality, urgent in its revelations, carries from gasp to gasp. These are challenging and captivating cadences. Worth every round.

—José Faus, *The Life and Times of José Calderon*
2025 Birdy Poetry Prize Judge

Catherine Anderson's poetry in *Afloat* brings us moments of luminosity, as in "Heard on the Street," about a bellringer who climbs the spiral stairs to a small belfry to play, of all things, "Love Me Tender," for those lucky listeners on the street below. There are any number of beautiful surprises in *Afloat*, like cutting rhubarb with "leaves larger this year than our two heads / put together," or buying roses and lilies at the grocery store during the pandemic. Anderson is able to turn almost everything we do into a ritual full of spiritual meaning: "Leaving port in the fog, / the captain chanted / the cloud-carved islands / we passed in the bay, each one / a breath—my mother gone, / my father gone—the captain's / voice fading as we hit / the open sea."

—Brian Daldorph, *Kansas Poems*

The speaker in *Afloat* is at once the girl "irritated /
by gravity, a lunar tug on my carved waist," her own
mother reaching for Marlboros, and every woman with
her "dark-petaled star." Dreamy, associative prose
vignettes at the center of the book—an "almanac" of the
pandemic—explore the deserted way we found ourselves
then, rendered as "the shoe heel of Amelia Earhart . . .
the eyetooth of Robinson Crusoe." Catherine Anderson's
expansive and deeply ethical poems consider what needs
mending, the wildernesses we have all crossed to get
where we are, and how to navigate our animal selves,
whose lot it is to both "swerve from dying" and to "meet
the dog / we all know."

—Rebecca Hart Olander, *Singing from the Deep End*

Afloat is a chronology from a writer not afraid of
universal themes. "How often I avoid the truth /
even as it arrows my way," Anderson writes. "I
resemble all women," she says and maps a life from
girlhood to maturity—a woman holding a handful
of stars ("Boylston Street Station"). With lyricism
and generosity, Anderson concludes with a blessing,
"Everyone you want to bless / could fill the planet—and
so you begin . . ."

—Cathryn Essinger, *The Apricot and the Moon*

AFLOAT

Catherine Anderson

MEADOWLARK PRESS

established 2014

EMPORIA, KANSAS

Meadowlark Press, LLC
meadowlarkbookstore.com
P.O. Box 333, Emporia, KS 66801

Afloat

Resale and Bulk Orders: For details, contact the publisher at
info@meadowlark-books.com.
https://www.meadowlarkbookstore.com/resale-and-bulk-orders

Cover Art and Design: Rosalie Krenger, Meadowlark Press

Author Photo: Robert Cole

Interior Design: Natalie Wolf and Linzi Garcia, Meadowlark Press

Font: Century Schoolbook

POETRY / American / General
POETRY / Women Authors
POETRY / Subjects & Themes / Family

ISBN: 978-1-956578-82-9

Library of Congress Control Number: 2025944093

Also by Catherine Anderson

In the Mother Tongue (Alice James Books, 1983)

The Work of Hands (Perugia Press, 2000)

Woman with a Gambling Mania (Mayapple Press, 2014)

Everyone I Love Immortal (Woodley Press, 2019)

My Brother Speaks in Dreams: Of Family, Beauty & Belonging (Wising Up Press, 2022)

Table of Contents

I.

II.

III. Almanac

IV.

For the poets, the makers, and the healers

I.

I look down on my hand like an astonished
Fortune-teller, seeing the mortal flesh

—Muriel Rukseyer

Midnight on My Birthday

Night has settled, the moon high
over the rain gutter.

I walk naked through the rooms
of my house, feel my collarbone ferried

from shoulder to shoulder,
my breasts unloosed, brushed by a curtain.

Through a window I watch
my neighbor run his pale wolfhound

under the streetlights, their six legs
pumping as they turn a corner, then

disappear into the new leaves of the lindens.
I stand in this tender skin bestowed

by my mother who smoothed her palms
all over it, this woman who carried me

from a darkness known only to her,
into a light both of us could see.

Afloat

Easy to imagine the one you love
as a child—flushed skin, bright
hair, so like water running
through your fingers, eyes
agleam in their glance toward you.
This lover has your full attention,
the story about to begin, your hand
tracing the forehead, the soft plum
of a cheek, the beloved known
as only the beloved is known.
After "the pond," "box turtle,"
"those guys," your lover's eyes settle
on a bedroom window frame,
a smudge on the ceiling, the eyes
of a child at rest within the story,
the long exhaled breath of it.
The story will continue, but now
a breath it must take, your lover's mind
floating on its back in the pond, your lover
silent for a moment, arms spread wide
like a T, attempting the back float,
the technique that could save a life,
what every child learns first, reverent
in the positioning: face up, ears and hair
submerged in small tides of the water,
the swimmer taking careful breaths
with you, spotter and listener.
The one you love rests on the water's
skin, eyes shut, then open, the child
you see in that face, your lover
who will never drown.

Red Maples

I didn't yet know the scarlet soul of those trees,
dark boughs carrying us on the school bus

in loco parentis as we sat up front, the trees' woody
arms brushing smeared windows, the yellow

sides and black wheels of our ramble down
Moravian Road, past acreage turned over

for wheat and soybeans. Thirteen, fourteen, all praise
and bite, we were cradled samaras for weeks,

then flung with twigs and stubs along the shoulder.
We were loud, relentless. I was a girl, irritated

by gravity, a lunar tug on my carved waist, my aching
head, the clockwork of my ovaries still unpredictable

as I learned to game decades of female existence.
Yet the trees who loved me held back their judgment.

Once a spot missed my notice before I could turn
my skirt around. I stood up, and the boys in the back

of the bus broke into jeers. I was a girl standing like
a maple tree floating a thousand wings into the cosmos.

Growth, decline, then release, the soul asway
in a stand of trees. I didn't know it then.

Now that I do, I'd like to turn around and take a bow
to those boys for all the days I've lived under a drape

of sunlit green, then red, then gold, all the days
I've lived and lived and forgotten them.

Miniature Woman, Carved from Ivory, 17th Century

On viewing this Galatea laid inside
a velvet box, of course I think
of my own body, and the body
of my mother, and her mother before.
No one knows why the figure was made.
One theory is that physician apprentices,
gentlemen more familiar with the birth
of foals, were taught to remove
the ivory mound of the figure's abdomen
as you would untop a butter dish.
Inside they would see the beaded
intestines and further down, a piece
of red yarn curled to resemble
an umbilical cord within
the delicate cup of the simulated
uterus and shell of placenta.
Nestled inside the hollow
lay a carved infant's head
and body, smooth as the moon.
The gentlemen saw no vagina
in this figure, only a cleft between
the tiny bone-mother's legs
as they plucked out the infant
with blunt, ink-stained fingers.
Because the anatomy was imprecise,
the figure could have been
merely decorative, shown off
in the parlor after dinner.
Standing over the ivory figure
in its box, were these men wrestling

Aristotle's argument that the soul
lives separate from the body?
Were they keen to know how
to stanch despair or halt life's cruelties?
Surely they agreed on the laws of the wedge
and lever, on Paracelsus's belief
in the curative use of mercury and salt.
But could they comprehend how a woman's body
floats on a plane of time?
I wouldn't blame their fumbling
if I knew they were awestruck
by female existence,
or even startled as I am after
a shower, when I glimpse my own
silk interior and realize I resemble
all women in that dark-petaled star,
from which every human has emerged.

Every Sparrow Fallen

My mother's mother was banished from her home
after giving birth out of wedlock.
The baby boy was taken from her and placed
in a Hell's Kitchen orphanage.
During the pandemic of 1918, she came back
to New York City as an army nurse
to work at the Embarkation Hospital.
I've known her only from photographs.
When I think about her then, I see her
counting rolls of bandages and vials of blood,
carrying water to soldiers in their beds,
and later, as it would be her job, I see her walking
among the bodies lining the morgue. A sign
on the door she opens: *Do not enter, do not touch.*
Every sparrow fallen, the city gray as a knife blade.
Sometimes I imagine a boy about the same age
as my grandmother's abandoned son
would be. He's waiting outside
the bronze doors of the hospital.
He watches a mule-hitched wagon lead
one coffin after the other over the rail tracks
to a graveyard. At the turn of dusk,
he sees her come down the steps,
starched nurse's cap fixed
to her bun, red cape flared
like a burning wing.

Office Hours

Of all earthly birds my favorite
is the brown thrasher—
rushing through dense shrubs
like a housekeeper, pitching twigs
and leaves as she sweeps the ground.
Every spring I watch them
from my office window, weeds high,
forming a kind of blind.
When Elena stops by to tell me how
she and her husband, an American
studying in her hometown of Volgograd,
first fell for each other, I stop watching
and listen. He saw her curls backlit
by the sun and brought her an armful of roses.
She liked the full sail of his mouth.
Without love, don't our faces evaporate
like water? Elena's hair falls in two
neat ropes the honey color of my desk.
Our talk then switches to error: how we
carry its scent home each night after work
on our raincoats, a fragrance of clarity
wrought, then mottled. We agree
on another error: The Virgin Mary's
leather belt worn to gather her sky-blue
robes, now on display in a storefront
church, tears of the faithful clouding the glass.
Of love and belief, who knows?
Each day we bend to our paperwork,
Elena and I, sheltering children
skinned by belts, working for the day
belting comes to an end.
That day could start a new beginning,

like the miracle of Thecla, I venture,
the Byzantine virgin thrown to lions
who refused, one day, in unison, to devour
her and laid their thick tongues on her face
and licked her back to consciousness.
Have you noticed that any time two people
meet, sooner or later the talk turns to animals?
Like the talk of trees, a way to avoid other horrors.
A red fox leaping bushes by the grade school,
a possum swerving through backyard mint.
Don't rush a decision, I tell Elena.
In college, I searched for dark
places, like the back of a parked circus
truck where a tiger paced its padlocked cage.
He met my eyes, smelled my face.
I shiver at another thought: chickens pecking
away at the tiniest one—the runt,
the untouchable, rump bald as a light bulb.
Killing a chicken is a female rite of passage
in the Midwest, I tell Elena,
yet I know a woman who used to keep
rescued chickens, calling them "my girls"
and letting them play ball with chickpeas.
An unforgivable error in some circles
was to talk of animals in the same breath
as humans, "My soul struck a deer." *No.*
I tell Elena to take her time, think it over.
We are rare women who have never killed
a chicken or given birth. We could talk
of love forever and never realize the hours,
like a homecoming of swifts, asleep
as they fly, winging the steel-swept clouds.

Sylvia Plath in the Night Realm

A few ways we could understand her—
think how she just missed
Dylan Thomas, launched straight off
to the Whitehorse Tavern after
the end of his reading.
In her lucent eye, she saw
them both raise a foamy glass
to the muse of fracture and revolt.

How to fire it, how to keep it,
she'd ask the poet, once she caught up
with him, blocks ahead
in his canter through the Village.
Their dialogue, in her mind—
straight up, swift—sprung by chance
on the street, the two whispering
their griefs, not as lovers, but as passing
gods of the night realm.

Or remember how hot
it was that summer in Manhattan,
the end of her apprenticeship
and its bridled fissure of art from life.
Remember the hotel rooftop where
everything changed. She peeled
off the tight lingerie and silk hose
under her skirt and threw it all
to the muggy wind.

Afternoon in Guanajuato

If I knew the street, I would show you where
I once found Antonio Machado's golden
spine of poems set in Gothic type,
laid out in a market bin to pick up
and hold like a ripe mango.

If I could show you how the sound of poetry
spoken in any language becomes
as sacred as love, you would see me
carry those poems in the small
cradle of my arms down the tight
streets of the old mining town
placed like a silver bowl
on a table between the high
mountains of Central Mexico.

I sat down in a café among others
to read these pages shipped
from Madrid, the volume
stitched with the thick
string used by a butcher
to tie a pound of meat.
Inside I found jasmine
and roses, a silence
to slit the sky.
Though the poet's griefs
were not mine,
I felt the mineral shadow
of a tongue incarnated as salt,
words cut into planes of stone.

I read quietly like the nun
on a train in one of his poems,
a young woman whose face
held back everything she felt.

Spring

My black jeans off, I'm sitting
in one of those white plastic chairs
that cradles your hind end
like a sugar scoop, my thighs
covered by a piece of old brocade
the tailor passed to me as he turned away
with my chalk-marked skirt billowing
gardenias, the one that cuffs the back
of my calves in a breeze but now lies
resplendent on the ironing board under
the tailor's hand as he pushes aside
a pin cushion the size of an orange,
and lifts one of two irons next to
a pair of metal shears the moment
I fear a water bottle will topple because
a one-eyed calico cat whose name
I know to be Agnes happens to walk
between the water and the scissors,
just before the final press of the newly
hemmed skirt of petals and stems, the one
I anticipate skimming not my calves
but a little shorter, to crest the top
of the knees once the alteration
is complete, this second day of April
in the year of our Lord 2022 when
I look past the rose calendar still showing
the month of March and the black
and white photograph of a Shetland pony
in a bowler hat, and wonder how long
beauty will last in the world, not knowing
the answer, but just thinking of my skirt,
how soon I'll put it on and twirl a little
for the final measure, then wear it
home instead of my jeans.

Let Us Now Praise Famous Women

Almost holy, their steam a cumulus wondrous.
A young woman I know named Emilia once worked
in the low-lit backroom of a Michelin restaurant,
where she pieced together a mock Carabid beetle
from marinated apple skins and sugared
orange peels for diners to take home
in a bamboo box as a late-night desert.
She was told not to laugh, though the beetle
was overpriced and tasted like beer nuts.
Not the penny wages, not the bad light,
but the laugh gag finally got her. At the end,
Emilia staged her exit interview to look like a wake,
herself laid out in queenly robes of cigarette butts
and oyster shells atop a packing crate.

If not praised, then damned, so I saint them
without beatification, I saint them
without knowing all their personal miracles
behind a barista counter or buried in a kitchen.
I overdo it—that's my generation.
But aren't young women bionic? And what
a re-run! Think the '68 Miss America Pageant,
a stack of bras ready to be smoked,
and across the Atlantic, tomatoes and white flour
hurled at beauty judges. Tomorrow
they dream like saints, mock beetles shoved
off the table as light touches a grease
splotch the sun passed by in the last eclipse.
I give no advice. I step back and watch.

At another well-lit place, there was the moment
my best friend realized men were both object

and obstacle, the café beginning to close, the help
brushing a broom over the blond parquet.
At a meeting over lunch she'd planned with two male
colleagues, they talked only to each other, slam-dunking
names into a mythical basket she couldn't see.
Wasn't she, the author of all clear ideas at this table,
the thinking Zeus from whose forehead ripe Athenas
were born? My friend's head ached, sunbeams gilded
the window. Nothing to lose, she swilled a glass
of tea the color of bourbon like a woman who steals
clubs or palms aces, while the tables were cleared,
the chairs up-turned in their places.

All praise for childless Aunt Doll, though if alive,
she wouldn't accept it, my great aunt the recipient
of a kind letter from a defeated Democratic
candidate, the letter read at her kitchen table
where she made Jell-O dessert and organized
for the Equal Rights Amendment in the pre-fab
house she built in Warrensburg, Missouri.
She liked debate, she liked to hear men talking,
my aunt a young reporter for the *Star-Journal*, the one
in the newsroom who knew how to win a White House.
If some women were meant to cool a man's self-lit blaze
on the campaign trail, then Doll in her linen suit
and logical short heels could have been one of those,
not wife, not lover, but sensible bucket of water.

Not far from Aunt Doll, Helen Beck was told
to be less "girly-girly," so she named herself
Sally Rand after a road atlas. Then she pranced
with two fluffy ostrich plumes on stage
at the Chicago World's Fair. Oh, to have been
a blue fly on the wall in that buzzing heat

of indignation. Jezebel! Tart! A frothy Niagara
of names those Bible-bearing people shouted.
Yet the burgomasters loved her, and so did
the veterans who sold pencils by the curb.
Feather sweep of her arms, over and through legs
and feet—knees in, fanny out. Back home
on a table, Bible pages lay open to a holy parade
of whores, beggars, thieves, and bores.

Their steam a cumulus wondrous, I saint them
without beatification, I saint them without knowing
too much. If I didn't the choices would be
to weep or elegize. That's my generation.
In truth, bras were not burned in 1968, the women
worried about danger to the protesting crowd.
About tomorrow, I'm not sure what to think.
Any day on the planet, a child of light, a child almost
holy, rides her bike home after getting a pixie cut
in the basement of retired beautician Mrs. Love.
On the girl's forehead, a pale lipstick smear, what
the girl's mother finds, parting the new bangs,
her daughter bearing a famous woman's gentle,
red-hued kiss, brief as the aurora borealis.

Knitting Lesson

All that is solid melts into air . . .
—Karl Marx

If only, that slogan lettered on a T-shirt,
a good wish for distributive justice.
Not the thin haze that still hovers
by my neighbor's chain link fence
when, decades after I left, she lit
a backyard grill to heat water for coffee
until one evening she was found cold,
coffee a frozen crust down her lap.
No heat that winter when taxes were due.
Borrowed water in a bucket.
A quick spit bath and can of beans
by the enamel sink with the rust marks,
where once each baby had been bathed,
the two infant girls I used to babysit, pink
mouths like petals, their legs bent froggish
as they kicked the water and grew
into the rose pajamas their mother
sewed on the Singer, tapped with one pedal.
No telephone for months the winter
neighbors found her like that,
no money for nitroglycerin pills.
As a kid, I couldn't master her Singer
though she tried to teach me how
to run a stitch, make a black pencil-line
skirt as tight fitting as hers. I would do
anything for her. We had better luck
with a pair of knitting needles, her hands
encasing mine, cigarette at her lip
as I followed one yarn loop through a circle

17

then caught again like hopscotch or Chinese
jump rope, the infinite chain I was so blind
to, throwing the yarn like someone
who believed any loop dropped
could be picked up and carried back,
any T-shirt rolled inside out until there it was,
what she told me to look for, that interlocking
squiggle of the jersey stitch—purl one side,
knit on the other, an equal distribution, that
shirt flung on the line to flap in the air.

The Great Lakes Are Not the Sea

Colors are the deeds and sufferings of light.
—Johann Wolfgang von Goethe

The window glass I look through appears
as calm water, a soft plate of sea
that will not break.

I often think about how the mind seeks
its own harbor, how blue permeates
the spectrum of color
with distance.

One year we moved away
from the lakes that made our home,
from my grandmother to the north,
from my silent middle brother
in an institution for children
called back then by a name
I refuse to repeat.

In one last visit with my grandmother,
I watched her mend a bedsheet,
white thread pulled
by her tiny needle under a lamp
in the heat of day.
She took care of what little
she possessed.
She taught me to wash only
the wilted part of my clothes—
the underarms, the crotch—
then dry them on a coat hanger
over the tub.

All our lives we list further away
from who we think we are.
The glass I look through
turns inland, a blue-melded gray
moving as one body, small laps
of wind rather than tides,
yet the illusion of tides,
the way glass changes what we see
when caught by the eye.

In the institution, my brother learned to sing
the letters of the alphabet.
Years later he was returned to us
by the state of Michigan.
I am not proud of this story.
Childhood can never be repeated
and the Great Lakes are not the sea
but a shimmering error
I carry with me.

To Fold Like Marie Kondo

Open your drawer and touch a scarf.
Feel the smooth-as-silk polyester against your skin,
how it swallows geography, outwits commerce,
fake silk bought for you as a gift
from London's Liberty hours before take-off,
the pattern a paisley print seen in a migraine aura—
orange-sparked wheels and teal lightning.
As you fold, think of the product of silkworms
the fabric imitates. Thousands of insects beat
the tropical night, chewing bushels of white
mulberries carried from orchard rows
by someone's aunt who moves like clockwork
to keep these larvae fed, to quicken spewed fibers
spun from metamorphosed bodies.
Note that the ancient economy
of an animal's work becomes no match
for machine strands of polyfabric—
light-weight, wrinkle-free—the exact cloth
for school uniforms, for dress shirts,
what you and your mother cheered, throwing
the ironing board down the stairs.
Touch that fabric with no life-cycle other than
its refusal to decompose. Press it
to your skin, let it catch your cuticles.

For Allen Ginsberg's Mother

Naomi, who smiled to the moon,
her six dark hairs on the wen
of her breast, the pink nightgown
she wore in the Bronx, her lentil soup made
for God, in his sadness.
A woman who conceived her son in a flash
of light so minute *all the hills*

echoed, echoed as the universe

continued its brilliance and despair, a sharp bolt
lost to a hymn. For the teenage Allen who
stayed home to save her, for brother
Eugene with tears in his eyes.
When we die, we become an onion, a cabbage . . .
their mother said.
Things lost—past, gone, *caw caw*

Seventeen-, eighteen-years-old, soon to leave
our own mothers, we stood listening
one night to Allen chant William Blake
outside the Jewish Community Center
with its ark-pointed roof raised to the sky—

And all the hills echoed, echoed
as a balm lifted trees—

O strange Naomi.

How to sing the poetic, how to make an edifice
of love and press it into permanency.

The Voice of Lorraine Hunt Lieberson

> *The ear of the ear, the eye of the eye . . .*
> *—The Kena Upanishad*

Her beautiful lust and then descent, carried
beyond time, a voice cased in light,

a climb toward what felt like the stratosphere
in those arias of Handel on a winter night.

What to hold, what to lose—I heard
her cancer appeared on raven's wings,

in the sense no one saw it coming
from such height.

A woman's breasts—part hers, part universe.
She continued to sing

the silver breath of each note.
She sang on her deathbed.

Instead of asking *why*, as I once did,
I ask, *who*

is that invisible one?
The ear of the ear, the eye of the eye.

Bears

I stand in the forest waiting, just another woman on Earth
about to lose it all. For hope, I study the cracks in clouds,
the slow motion of water on leaves, the light
it holds through the hours—Earth in its rotation
and revolution, both.
When Elizabeth Marshall Thomas was young and alone
in her dorm room, she'd spend evenings looking
through her microscope.
She once saw a monster in a speck of swamp water
and fell off her chair.
With one eye on the lens, she chased the speck
as it moved along the slide.
It grew small, smaller, then larger, then small.
She touched it with a needle and lifted it to the light
for a view in three dimensions.
It was round and stuffed, resembling a toy bear.
Smaller than the head of the needle, it slipped
back on the slide "unfazed by the experience," she wrote.
She saw a snout, two eye spots, the form bilateral.
A tardigrade, or water bear, it had "a nice face," she wrote.
Two bulges on the side probably meant cubs.
A female, like me, she thought.
In the summer of 2019, thousands of dehydrated tardigrades—
part of a lunar library on the Beresheet spacecraft—
crash-landed on the moon.
Since the beginning of electricity, we are moths seeking
the light we invent.
I think we have run out of inventions.
To feel like a child I sit down to watch TV.
And again, bears: *their witness and torpor*, almost
a line taken from a fable read before sleep, as if a bear

had curled up in a corner of my room, snoring.
We are encircled by animals—small, large, larger, smaller.
Seen, unseen. The water bear has its own genus.
A cave was found with a mother bear and her new cubs.
The forest ecologist anesthetized the mother, then listened
for the wails of her cubs as she fell
into unconsciousness.
She breathed deeply. This was a good sign.
The forest a carved atrium on the TV screen, the cubs wailing.
The forest ecologist pinned a clip to each cub's ear,
the ear not sensitive to pain.
Other forest ecologists came from behind the camera crew
and took over weighing the cubs,
then maneuvering the big mother to be checked.
A voice off camera: The health of bears
is a measure of the health of the forest.
The voice: If the little bears weigh a lot, they've been eating.
If they eat, their mother eats.
If each bear has enough to eat, the forest is in balance.
One stands for many, a measure of the whole—
O bears, O forest, O Earth—
I snap off the TV and the screen turns dark, like water.

II.

When you have left the river you will hear the war.

—Muriel Rukeyser

The Clay Bowl

In the middle of your life, you asked
for something round to hold

your terrible thoughts.
You were given orange-blue fire

to carry, a trinity of flames
in the shape of a bowl, dry

as paper at the fingertips,
a handful of earth fired at the horizon.

No one asked what you grieved
though its mark was real.

You burned from particle to ash.
Your sorrow resembled all other sorrows.

Stolen

In my life, I've taken it all—the meat,
the skin, the root, the water, the petroleum
that fuels my going, steals
the air from someone else.

I've taken the feathers, the magnetic
bones, the gold,
the healing mint, the willow bark.

I would have stolen refracted sunlight
in the wing of an indigo bunting
to sketch a picture, if I could.

I cannot think of a word for this,
yet there must be one.

Without even knowing, I stole a bit of cobalt—
the demon element
powering the lithium-ion battery
of cell phones, mined by children working
in the open pits of the Democratic Republic of Congo.
Cobalt in its other form shines
with the blue pigment of its name.
In an art store, I found a thin, sharp
pencil in this color for the shade
it casts in shadow.
I thought that was all cobalt was, a color.
I bought it to enhance the blue
throat of my bird.
There is no word, no equivalent—
to draw a bird, to steal from a child.

Seven Sketches

1. The Letter B Pronounced at the End of the Word Bomb

A plosive sound he made with his lips
pushed together and then pulled
apart, finished with an audible puff,
quick into our conversation.
I wished we could have said more.
I wanted to know how they survived,
how he covered his small son
with the full length of his body,
but all I heard when he spoke
was that slight sound erupting
again, like the first time decades ago
I heard someone describe
a different place, another war,
those persistent days not knowing
when it would stop.

2. A Soft CH *in the Word* Stomach

It should be pronounced that way,
he argues, in homage
to that tender bowl
we all carry
waiting to be filled.
He remembers it hollow
in the days of famine,
when the first hint of his own starvation
could be measured by how
easy it was to ring an index finger
around his wrist to meet his thumb,
when he was a young man,
lucky so far
not to be blind from hunger,
when he could still turn
over a wet log in the forest
to find something to eat.

3. *The Color Gamboge*

Capture of the hue became
the country's first betrayal,
for who doesn't want
to possess a color valuable
as gold, whose sheen
rivals the sun, the origin
of all color?

The bright yellow
of Lord Krishna's clothes
in Indian miniatures,
or the rattan yellow of robes
worn by Buddhist monks,
gamboge was a fixture
in the paintbox of Turner
who flooded his canvas
with the hue as if
he were tapping the sky
for its reverberating light.

In the forest, raw gamboge
was collected for years
from the *Garcinia hanburyi*,
relative of the mangosteen,
its bark sliced so gum
ran from the trunk
into hollow bamboo poles.

In another betrayal, but not
the country's last, during
the Southeast Asian wars
of the twentieth century,

people were killed extracting
gamboge, the forest
seeded with landmines.

At the height of war,
when gunfire blasted
the bamboo poles
to the ground,
crumbled gamboge
became mixed with bullet
casings to create not gold,
not sunlight, but pigment
suffocated by mud,
never to glisten again.

4. The Word Ache, with Its Own Sadness

Once a rhyme with the word *match*
in Middle English, that soft
ch at the end again,
hovering like a touch.
Through the ages of English,
the word also meant a longing after loss,
the remainder of pain.
In the plural, if you can imagine
multiple losses—a home,
a country, a family—you hear
a word that comes close
to the sound of *ashes*,
yet the *e* always silent
because aches are imperceptible
to the one sitting beside the other
who yearns in daylight,
who hesitates to speak
among strangers.

5. The Weight of Light

The immigration lawyer has just read
a post about the asylum judge
who denied the man
with a paralyzed leg
and six children.
She's learned about the interpreter's
parched throat rendered voiceless
the day of the hearing, not
from shock but from stiff air
deadening the courtroom.
Immigration lawyers are given
little time, but she would like to stop
a moment, and slowly ask
these questions to anyone listening—
What is the weight of light?
Does it fall like gravity or drop
like mercy from heaven
to the place beneath?

A chattering boy in a bright amber
cap waits with his mother
in a room of mops and boxes.
Everyone who comes through these doors
has crossed a wilderness somewhere
on Earth to get here.
This morning each desk
in the office heavy with paper,
and through the window blinds,
small blades of fractured light.
A water bottle rolls across the floor.
A giggle from the little boy who watches
the doors and windows, yet may never
remember the woman he will soon meet,
the sound of her voice, his mother's anxious lilt.

6. Causeway After a Rainstorm, Angkor Wat, Cambodia—2000

As they approach the entry
to the great temple,
a mother and her child
walk hand in hand
over stones silvered by rain.

The sky above them opens—
two small figures
measured by light—the child
a luminous dream
carried by ancestors
into the silence
of water and earth.

7. *The Word* Samsara

If you were trying to understand a time from the past
and how it repeats in the present,

if you were trying to comprehend the whole
spectrum of beauty and evil on Earth,

and if you were not ready to utter the word
hope, even in your mind,

you would be wise to think about rain
falling outside the window of a rented house

converted into a Buddhist temple where
a Cambodian monk sat, his golden robe

crossed over his left shoulder, the right one bare
in deference to the senior monk near him.

You'd remember the monks came here
to heal their own people and the people

they lived beside. You'd recall the long, sacred
chant, the green and orange colors

of the temple, the children who came out of the rain
with their parents to this modest house set among others.

If you reflected long enough and recalled everything—
the elders who closed their eyes as they prayed,

the families who brought bowls of rice for the monks
and waited for them to eat first, after prayers—

if you thought deeply,
you might use the word *samsara*

from *The Katha Upanishad* to describe the phenomenal
world and its cycle of birth, death, and rebirth,

a word whose Pali and Sanskrit roots
suggest the idea of wandering as we all do,

each on our own eternal wheel of desire and loss.
You would be grateful to those monks,

and you would try hard to grasp the word,
if only for a moment.

Invention of the Helicoptor

After the accident a man holds
a woman in tight embrace.
A police helicopter hovers, the blades
a panic-attack sweep as it lands the way
its inventor designed—straight down,
bull's eye, how a hummingbird lights
on a hibiscus in July, having evolved
with such slow motion to blend
with the mirror-red-blue-green
of what surrounds it.

You could say the hummingbird
is a verb of being,
a copula reflecting its own origin:
the hummingbird, the nectar-rich world.

And the helicopter, a steel-bullet body
of gray-and-brown-spotted camouflage,
the military hue a man sees every day
waking up, what he's known since boyhood,
lining up his soldiers, the pattern
of a T-shirt, a backpack.
All this a copula too, as the helicopter
equals the danger of the world,
a reminder that lasts a lifetime—little boy,
bazooka raised to the sky, eyes closed, then open.
Like the man they tell him he should be,
he walks out of the dream into a gunshot city
in July, ambulance lights swirling in the black air,
heavy with sirens and the scent
of burned plastic.

The colors of camouflage
spread and devour all they touch.

The woman on the street knows
the silhouette of grief the two
of them make, her arms
entwined with the arms
that have found her,
like a hummingbird touching a bloom.

The God Within the Stranger

Consider the one who travels among us,
who hears a multitudinous chant

in crumbly, honey-laced bread,

who looks at the rain and sees
a parade to fog the heart.

So far from home, she can taste the village.

We revere the gods for the mirror of their eyes:
They are who we are in disguise.

The street she wanders, a burst,
a plethora: How do I live?

What food can I find, where do I sleep?
How do I write my mother?

Diana's Arrow

How often I avoid the truth
even as it arrows my way,

sleek & unsubtle. Last summer
the city abandoned the public pool

I loved with its flowered filigree facing
Cedar Road, built before cities rose up

to spark their necessary fires, built when
a Black child who wanted to swim here

would have been barred from entering.
But that was the past, I told myself.

For months I watched the pool fade
away with the finches & lilac trees

until it turned stagnant, pigeon feathers
scumming the tiles. Whatever injustice

a long time ago can't happen again,
I told myself. Nearby, I saw oak leaves

had settled like a helmet of ash on a statue
of Diana—protector of children,

women, all living things—the deity
whose arrow never misses.

You'd think she might have tired
of the chase, that she'd had

enough of human evasion, yet plucked
from her heavy quiver I could see

another arrow, one she would send to arc
the sky & pierce my heart until I got it.

Turnspit

curtailed dog fit only to run in a wheel
                                    —William Shakespeare

Perhaps this is how everything
turned ugly: A slaughtered pig
had to roast on open flames
before it could be eaten.
A man had to pick up a squat
dog and set him inside
a wooden wheel fit high
on the master's kitchen wall, hot
coals thrown to the dog's feet
to make him run quick inside
the spinning cage connected
to a pulley turning a spit
of pork on the fire.

I can't get that scene out of my head—
dizzy dog turned nasty, ready
to bite—*canis vertigus*, what Linnaeus
named the breed—short with crooked
legs, dusky tail flailing smoke
that drifted over stone, over
the bent head of a man not permitted
to eat in the same room as the family
of this house while the wheel
on the wall moved faster
and faster until the dog fainted
and the meat was done.

Escape

Beyond the tips of its brown ears
are fields swallowed by sky,
by shovelfuls of rain.

In one account, a month before plague
struck Nuremberg, Dürer captured
a young hare, its coat past molting.

In the background of the portrait—
blank space—no oak leaves,
no timothy grass,

only raked strokes of black on gray,
the captured animal's fluid heat
and fascia, waiting to leap.

Who among us hasn't waited
with held breath to make
our own escape?

For hours the hare watched him
from a cage on the drawing table.
I am sure of this.

Young hare, wild hare,
in the bead
of your eye is a window.

Born After the War

On my father's knee in a Detroit tavern
I listened to the voices of his friends—
men who didn't hang out with cops
but drank with priests,
men who drove six-axle rigs
and hunted mushrooms
after clocking out at the plant,
men who sold rugs from the trunk
of their cars, who cut beef
and pork with knives
passed from father to son,
men who spoke English that began
with a traveling gust then grew
louder like hardware carried
in the bed of a truck or car chains
rattling in winter, like the blast
of whole streets set on fire when
people are rounded up and murdered
on the land where they were born—
men who drank the cold vodka
of memory and forgetfulness,
who blessed me with calloused hands
brushing the top of my head, who believed
my eyes would never see the worst
of these mentioned things
but would know others.

III. Almanac

Like two golden birds perched on the selfsame tree,
Intimate friends, the Ego and the Self
Dwell in the same body. The former eats of the tree of life
While the latter looks on in detachment.

—The Mundaka Upanishad

1.

Months have slipped by since my last visit to the sea. Laid down like a dinner plate on a table, the sea spreads north of the Missouri River, beyond the river bend into the plains. Driving along, all I see as far as the horizon is deep indigo. And between the trees, glimpses of water, still as an empty shelf. The sand lining the shore is white with many bathers running in and out, chasing the waves. I never learn the name of this sea, or the bay where people gather. I simply expect it to appear thirty miles north of the city. Some people enjoy surfing, but I stay out of the deep end. No intimate of mine has ever joined me, but I do recall talking to people as we waited for the tide to come in. I got my toes wet, then my feet and ankles and finally, I was full in the water. A teenage boy laughed at me. A dog came to shore when I did and shook itself from head to tail. The days are usually sunny, but I don't mind an overcast hour or two as I sit alone wrapped in a towel on a low-slung lawn chair in the sand and read my book. If the towel I bring is big enough, I shape the end of it like a hood to pull over my head when it starts to rain. There is an interesting lane with rowhouses on one side, facing the shore. They have a kind of Netherlandish look—tilted, tall, multi-colored. I walk around and around them each time I visit. The predominant colors are yellow and red, the colors of tulips. I woke easily in the morning, returning from this dream. We were in day one hundred of the pandemic.

2.

As I am a person drawn to the sound of words, what struck me first was the melody. The name *corona* pronounced in three evenly spaced vowels, two repeating, and the ending sound, "ah," like a breath released. The visual image the word creates defines it—a crown, a halo of light, a yellow circle rounding the outside of a sunflower, the ringed aura of the aurora borealis, or as I've learned, the faint glow of a released electrical charge. The sound of its loveliness soon became a decoy for its lethality. I have called it "the coronavirus" in my emails and Zoom encounters, knowing full well I should use the scientific name crowned by the World Health Organization: COVID-19—its sound more hostile, bare-toothed, and true. I have to give in. The virus's prickly pin spikes have already pierced.

3.

An ensemble of shops along a street. The places
I've escaped and then returned to just on the edge
of waking: the barber shop with the numbers games
my father remembered; the florist and hair salon; the
shop with the Russian cobbler and irritable tailor.
The Russian cobbler's daughter fell in love with the
tailor's son. The tailor's son shared the same birthday
as the gas station owner. The gas station owner was
the one my father sought when I took his keys away
because he insisted on driving without a license. One
resemblance of a place is its unconscious authority, a
secret mental anchor. Eight stores bric-a-brac down
the street. I come and go, visiting there only a few
times before waking.

4.

Albert Camus's novel, *The Plague*, was strongly criticized in its time. Some claimed Camus was not faithful to the act of resistance against the Nazis. The plague metaphor failed, they said, because the specific damage the microbe caused was personal, not communitarian. They claimed Camus had rejected history, and in so doing, justified individual solitude. In a letter, Camus defended his art: "Far from being installed in a career of solitude, I have, on the contrary, the feeling that I am living by and for a community that nothing in history so far has been able to touch." History, community, touch. One evening on TV I saw windows filled with faces of those who didn't want solitude—the old, the middle-aged and young adult, the ill and recovering. For those thrown into despair because they had lost a parent or a spouse, no one could say that being alone was their choice. The first person to succumb in our city was a school superintendent. His son said he had just come home from a magician's conference when he became ill. His father was someone who pulled scarves out of ears, floated the Queen of Hearts in the air, took off his hat to show a dove perched on his head.

5.

I was alone, working from home. I didn't want a
broken thread in my pantleg hem to further unravel. It
had been raining all day and now, the last hour before
sunset, light poured from the parted clouds. I found
a needle and thread. I set my leg with the torn hem
on my knee, bunched my pant leg and tilted it toward
the window to see what I was doing. I could just make
out the texture of the fabric against the dark thread.
Birds appeared on a branch of the dogwood outside the
window, a male cardinal and its gray-green mate, both
flitting through the leaves, chasing each other. Soon
the thread between my fingers balled up in my palm.
I had been entranced by the birds. Giving up on the
slipshod hem, I tied a minuscule knot and snipped it
with kitchen shears. The male flew to a low wire and
began calling, calling, to mark its territory, a border
I could not see or even guess. I put away the shears,
blades facing down in the cracked jar from an art fair
ten years ago. I didn't want to misplace things and
tried hard to keep track of where I last laid my pen,
my eyeglasses, the book I was reading. Later, I would
navigate through the rooms of my house collecting
those things without even thinking, like a bird steered
by the fixed senses of its species.

6.

What I've wanted to say, many times, has been impossible. Often, I've been permanently tongue-tied, missing the chance to ask a question or force an opinion. Minutes later, I could be at the bottom of the staircase, my handcuffed tongue now loosed, speaking the words that should have been spoken fifteen minutes ago. At the Starbucks counter, I wore a mask. The glass case opened to food: solid loaves of bread and rectangular pastries as if cast in rubber, or even—imagine—a 3D printer. I edged closer to ask the barista if the food was real, real in the sense I could reach my hand through the plexiglass and pick it up and eat it. A warehouse I once visited was filled with artificial food: slices of lemon meringue pie, German chocolate cake and rows and rows of rubber-cast bagels, pumpkin bread, an egg and bagel sandwich, and deep brown brownies. I had no desire for these, at the warehouse. At Starbucks, though, the pastries delighted me and I wanted the barista to talk about their origins and stories. She shook her head, not understanding my question. I walked home with my coffee.

7.

I know I am deathless, **wrote Walt Whitman.** For some reason, this statement made me wonder about the word *desert* in the phrase "desert island." I learned it's an archaic form, related to the adjective *deserted.* Today I confess I am *desert.* I am wind, I am sand. I am the shoe heel of Amelia Earhart. I am the eyetooth of Robinson Crusoe. I am Tom Hanks's face-mashed Wilson. I am the crux of rival fly-lords Ralph and Jack. I am tears, bones, dust. Ha.

8.

The body split from the head, the head split from the nose. Nose, mouth, and chin subtracted, in a mask, now familiar as clothing. Yet, out of the body we still prepare for embarkation, we gesture, we perambulate through the hours. The plagues named in the Haggadah on Passover—locusts, frogs, lice, darkness, ones that come up out of nowhere to shatter our world—transfix us more than ever. As animals, we work tirelessly to avoid death. This is our lot: to eat, procreate, and swerve from dying. Some days we'd like to set it all in reverse.

9.

From a poem by Rumi:

Here's the new rule: Break the wineglass,
and fall toward the glassblower's breath.

10.

One morning I realize I've grown accustomed to my new habits of work. I turn on the laptop, settle with a mug of tea, then bend my screen as needed to begin a meeting. The display of colorful faces within their squares appear like a clutch of baseball cards or holy cards of the saints. These are the people I know. I should be participating, I should be working, but the whole time my mind takes a bus ride with their wavering smiles, bowed heads and frowns. I traverse what has become a vast city of solitude and repetition along vacant streets and wind-swept corners. Tomorrow will be very much the same.

IV.

I stood in a crowded street that was live with people,
and no one spoke a word, and the morning shone.

— Muriel Rukeyser

Heard on the Street

My friend the bellringer
climbs up to the small belfry
of St. John's overlooking
the square, the spiral stairs ascending,
descending, like the riddle
he bellows down the stairwell—
what goes up and down
all day without moving?
The rock pigeons who hear him
don't budge from their roost
on the ledge.
At the top it's possible to see
new buds on the elms,
and between the branches,
a squirrel's nest.
The sky a blue plum this morning.
The bellringer and I haven't
spoken in years.
He takes off his belt
to replace for a moment
the worn rope of the tenor bell.
Not to lose his pants, he stops
to hitch up the waistband to his girth.
To sing when no one listens is an act of grace.
He reaches for the end of the tufted rope,
midway up what bellringers call
the sally where he makes a loop knot.
This is how he attaches the belt,
now ready to ring the notes
to the tune of *Love Me Tender,*
Love Me True, as if it were a hymn
and those of us walking the square
in love with something
we never knew.

The New Trees

At the end of day, cool air
parts the maples.
I grab the thin
box of my phone
for a walk through
the neighborhood.
I am my mother reaching
for a pack of Marlboros
to meet her friend
Maxine on the corner.
If smoke were a shadow
I would inhale
shadows, phone tilted
to my chin as I walk past
the new trees standing
in their new leaves,
arms akimbo.
I would watch for the light
from a neighbor's house
to signal—
come over, Shadow,
come talk to me.

A Wind Named Sam

When I open the door, wind zips
in like a dog who owns the place,
the dog I loved as a child but could not
pet because canine dermatitis
made the black and tan curls
of his Airedale coat redden
and flake, leaving brown flecks
of fur on our palms if
we stroked him, and if stroked,
the more he would scratch
with such good nature, tongue out,
an ecstatic look in his ebony eyes
as the rash spread in the hot
days of summer when the poor,
beautiful dog sought the cold porcelain
of an empty bathtub to lounge in,
shedding his cherubic
hairs, thumping his short tail
for anyone who came into
the bathroom carrying food
or water, telling him what a good dog
he was, born on the farm to parents
Jupiter and Venus, our dog Sam,
named after the only boss
my father liked, how smart Sam
was to find this cool spot,
how better things would be tomorrow
when the heat broke, and he could
chase the bears of his ancestors
in our backyard before coming
through the door again to teach
us how to love what we can't
touch, our dog in a twirl
of leaves and sticks as if
he owned the place.

Quotidian: On Five Photographs by Deanna Dikeman

1. *On a Ladder*

Sunday afternoon.
Newly mown grass
crests the air.
Your son stands on a ladder
splattered with paint, ready
to pass to your mother
the chrome screws
of the light fixture,
her palm open
to this child
no longer a child.
She lets him help her
now with rituals
of cleaning and replacing,
a reversal that begins
the rest of her life.
Soon he will present
the glass globe filled
with dried wings
she shakes out
before handing it back
to him so he can fit
the glass over the single
bulb fragile as an egg.

2. *How to Cut Rhubarb*

Trust me.
The leaves larger this year than our two heads
put together.
You'd lose a knife in the lap
of the grass, so sit here with me.
Grip the rhubarb stem in your hand
like a rope a puppy tugs.
Balance the leaf between your knees.
Draw your knife downward,
cut across the stem.
The first ten are endless.
Don't nick your leg.
With your last stroke
the veined leaf will break apart,
fall like water to your feet.
Trust me.

3. *The Visit*

He ascends the scratchy cloud
of the apple tree, your father
in his cap and quilted jacket,
hidden among the sculpted
crescents of the leaves,
the weighted boughs.

Each sure foot on the rungs
of the ladder, the same
wicker basket balanced below.
His whole life he has carried
tools from one place to the other.
Your whole life you have known him.
Yesterday you saw the apple bones
of his cheeks when he waved
as you came up the driveway.

His hands are obscured,
but you hear the hawk-beaked
clippers he opens and closes.
In this final harvest before
the frost, you make out
his bent elbow as he leans
into the branches that embrace
him, willing their fruit.

4. *Cleaning Jack's Grave*

If gravity is generous
let's gather to welcome
its intrusion

a force we can never escape
though we wish for kindness
a wide scatter

that spares no favorites
a power layered evenly
in descent like a cloud turned

fog wrapping the meadow
in May after days
of rain

the shovel we follow
so sure of its spiral
toward what

we've always loved
as our own deep
open-armed Earth

5. *Argument with Nostalgia*

They have come again as the taste of licorice.
A wonder each time this happens—

my friend who talks of animals and boats,
her father who stokes a charcoal grill

and later will teach us how to ring
a game of horseshoes deep

into the claret night. Why do they return
bearing their gifts for the folds

of my unguarded brain?
They are not even grieved

yet resemble the ones who are.
Get out of here! I command.

Take back the salt of this black candy,
the smoke of these charcoal-thick

streets. Like good obsessions,
they persist, saying, *Why deny us*

when you know
we would never leave you?

Morning Fog

so hungry it slides through
the open door,
passes by the kitchen,
the living room, like a traveler
come home,
turning corners until
it departs through the screen
of the back window above
the bed where my parents slept,
their heads tilted north.

The two now boxed, now silent,
buried on a common hill against
a sky brushing cloud intervals
that last, then fade.

When my father died, I carried paper
and glass to the basement.
When my mother died, I took to sea.
Leaving port in the fog,
the captain chanted
the cloud-carved islands
we passed in the bay, each one
a breath—my mother gone,
my father gone—the captain's
voice fading as we hit
the open sea.

A Winter Tune

We wot that our parents do but bear us into death.
A strange thing, that.
—Julian of Norwich

Because your mother would not
trill the word *forget* though
she knew how to sing
better than you.

Because the dust in your mother's house
was yesterday, one finger
brushing the end table
of curses under breath—
fallen ribbons scattered on touch.

Because the dust in your desk drawer
promised a tune bundled
in fantasia—graphite flakes
and eraser crumbs shadowed
by minnows in the reeds.

Dust with you always, carried
on your tongue, in your windpipe,
carried with the choir
you joined this winter, chuffing
through parking lot snow
in overcoat and boots,
dust you carry not for eternity
but in the voice of it.

Boylston Street Station

On a Tuesday night I come out of the snow
into what looks like the whole world
getting on a wooden escalator
from the last century creaking
in descent to the outbound platform
of cracked walls and rats
scrambling between the rails.
I haven't felt this cold underground
in a long time, so I'm struck
by ice crystals locked for a moment
to the woolen fibers
of our coats and scarves,
the odd relief I feel when warm
air rushes from the tunnel
to announce the arrival
of a Green Line car.
Then the swirl of puffy jackets,
the echo of boots scraping the threshold.
Subway doors close with a whoosh.
Eyes shut, faces fall with such trust,
the world at rest until the next stop.
The car screeches a half-circle turn,
nearly touches the glass booth
where a man sits at a desk under a clock.
I wave to him—one solitude regarding
the other—as he looks up
to catch my sleeve of melted stars.

Advice from Orpheus

To find what's lost, slip
through the shale cavern, past

the no-entry zone,
the too-late-to-be-saved gate,

down to the bottom
where you meet the dog

we all know barking
its sooty cough.

Pound the Earth into bits
of cake and plead

to the dark gods until
cracked notes stagger

from your throat like a scratch
of bats flapping

the stalactite walls,
slicing their coal shadows.

Return

Buffed as cherry wood,
my mother's brown eyes still
come back to me when I least expect.
The summer she lay dying
far away in another city,
I shared an office on the seventh
floor with two men.
One of them wore a bow tie
with a sweater vest, even in the heat.
The office was windowless.
I never knew the time of day.
In my mother's eyes, always a soft breeze,
like a curtain fluttering.
Her voice, too, rising in the middle
of a simple question, as if
struck by wonder.
I needed to see her, but when
to get away was not clear.
The lung cancer my mother had
was called oat cell. Under a microscope
it resembled the splayed shape of the grain.
As a child, I once plucked a strand
of oats from a field, spread out the husks
in my hand, then shoved them
deep into my pocket.
*We know we all die, but the mystery
is when*, said the man in the sweater vest.
When. In a whisper. I stared at the wall.
If my eyes began to well,
these men didn't see it.

On Viewing *Wing of a Blue Roller* by Albrecht Dürer

Melancholy elbow, sad shoulder blade
in the artist's study of the bird
on the table.

From beyond the sea the bird flew in,
a mark of blue edging
the greater coverts, feathers painted

that rare ultramarine.
The longer your eyes wander the painting,
the more you see the full body

of the bird come alive—its pectoralis
muscles wedging a sky the trees
make green, a trick

the eye teaches the mind
to accept. Beauty follows death,
a lesson forgotten each time,

then recalled, but not completely,
I say as we turn the pages
of this book about the artist,

trace our hands over the bent
wing, the partial bird
swept in blue.

To Draw a Bird

Begin with the bare slope
of the head, one light
pencil stroke before
the bird pivots.
The head like a small egg,
the oval eye patch, the beak that follows
the line of the eye.
The throat more alive than wings,
slender thread of graphite,
shaded gray.
Other parts—wingbar, flank, tarsus—
to be drawn as if the bird
would never stop breathing

but this can't be true.
Mark the smooth rag white
of the page to show
the pattern of feathers,
the curled talons on a branch.
Don't erase.

The monk's prayer
in the first eye flutter of morning,
a call to live deeply,
accept mortality, look at all beings
with attention.

First, to look.
The bird sits, then flies off.

Fat Tuesday at Our Local Aldi

My hair swept back in a silk
of red and yellow birds,
let me dance with my neighbors
before the Lord, chandelier loops
hanging from my ears,
gold threads flying down my jacket
cut above a petticoat grazing
blue-leather Tony Lamas, good
for stomping the melted grit
of winter, stepping
to the cornucopia of nested mangoes,
the random Cara Caras in season
for a blink, my boots in line
to follow a man in an orange
jumpsuit and cat ears,
the highways of our midbrain
plowed to the horizon
in what we call praise, this swerve
from lament to dance.
Tomorrow we turn to ash.

Dreams of the Other Dreamers

The New Year cleaves, then vanishes
with one brush of the hand—
impermanent as snow fallen
on the flannel back of the first-born
asleep by a window left open
to the slanted wind, the child forgotten
until the wakened parent stumbles
into the violet light of the room.
Who would believe how the child
was lifted up like a dream,
the snow swept off, cold dots
dropped, melted to nothing
on the wooden floor?

Now I am old, all I want to see
are stars—once alive, or *afire*,
a word burning as rich as the trick
to make us believe that when a star appears
in the night stream, it will never die.
On New Year's Eve my youngest brother
said that summer he finally found
our grandmother's grave.
He took the bus down Troost in the heat
to the cemetery where he searched
stone after sleeping stone sunk
into the grass. I touched his arm
as he told this story, my brother
the dreamer, awake among
all the other dreamers.

Flowers in a Time of Plague

Yellow roses on long, de-thorned stems,
soft-striped lilies with stamens curled
like a choir of questions.
Your cluster for me purchased swiftly
from the masked florist
weaving between buckets in the grocery
aisle of necessary items, a time when
chartreuse appeared, then fuchsia,
April-hued and fully saturated,
the greens rained green.
When we met, I embraced their shy leaves,
the multifoliate petals spilled
from the basket of your arms into mine
because we couldn't touch.
My curled proxies, my substitutes,
their beauty animate yet soon
to fade. I placed them upright
in a vase as you watched.

Does the Inertia of a Body Depend on Its Energy-Content?

Imagining ends of all kinds, I woke up early
and decided to read about the Chicxulub
asteroid bursting out of the Oort cloud to crash
the northern Yucatan Peninsula sixty-five million
years ago and kill off the dinosaurs, ending
any further procreation from that species
and making room for Homo sapiens
to eventually thrive and devour.
The Wiki entry was expansive when
all I wanted was the crystalline language
of weather, what I could feel on my face
like hailstones or straight-line winds.
When I leaned deeper into the void,
I realized Einstein's paper on relativity
could explain the sleeping Canada geese settled
along a bank of stones at the edge of the pond
where we walk. The inert geese always face
east, but when we approach them, they get up
with a burst of energy to angle their bulk
in the opposite direction, as if to give
a resounding *Yes* to that 1905 question.
A mind so homemade, so artisanal
as mine can point to geese, can dream up
any number of nouns to pair the word
"celestial," but cannot fathom
the order of magnitude or the loss of you
to me, the unthinkable notion I refuse
to consider, as hard to imagine as the intimacy
of dinosaurs, an insouciant Adam and Eve,
chewing fern leaves in paradise, not watching the sky.

To Make a Cloak

Spread a swath of linen on a table.
Imagine stars draped over
the night's round shoulders.

This will help you see stitches hidden
from most people's eyes.
Cross your needle with a ray of thread

and let it dangle. This is your hope, the slant
of your fast wrist as it pulls
a blanket stitch from one sturdy

border to the other.
You are never as lost as you are
years after the loss when it's clear

the gods have vanished.
And where have they gone, the people
you loved? Are they found among

the stones in the road?
Aesop said he watched a man clutch
his cloak against the wind until

the sun warmed the linen threads
of the garment and he shook it off
like an abandoned night.

Fall, Again

In the cabin hidden among northern firs
my friends and I agreed
that whoever sleeps
in the front room stokes
the stove through the night.
Lucky one, I lay swaddled in wool,
watching our fire roar
and fall in silhouette, great sweeps
of draft setting the blaze aglow.

We'd come north again to drink wine
and trade our tales, each of us
a year older and no one sad.

Hours before, I brushed aside brown
leaves to collect our kindling.
On the wind, the pine memory of Canada.
The sky above a bridge of deep
indigo spanning dusk and night.
On the ground, scattered pine needles,
sticks and cones, all loose, fitful.
I gathered these up, knowing
my promise and our necessity.

The Insomnia of Saint Symeon the Stylite

How his night resembles yours
when *chill stars spark*—

the nod off, then awake again
on the pitch of a roof,

the slab of a pillar.
Everyone you want to bless

could fill the planet—
and so you begin: Blessed are they

who sleep in clouds.
Blessed are they robbed by crows.

Blessed are they who rest, who fight,
who travel with rain packed

in a satchel. And blessed are they
who stop to brush ice crystals

off the cloak of Saint Symeon
in their wander, counting the night.

Notes

In "For Allen Ginsberg's Mother," the words "all the hills echoed" are from William Blake's "The Nurse's Song." Details in the first stanza and other italicized words are from Allen Ginsberg's *Kaddish*.

In "The Voice of Lorraine Hunt Lieberson" and in the epigraph of "Almanac," the quotations from the *Upanishads* are translations by Eknath Easwaran from his *The Upanishads, Translated for the Modern Reader*.

For "The Color Gamboge," the word gamboge is a corruption of the Latin for Cambodia. The epigraph refers to a description by Victoria Finlay in *Color, A Natural History of the Palette*.

"Causeway after a Rainstorm, Angkor Wat, Cambodia —2000" is based on the photograph of the same name by John McDermott.

The poem by Rumi referenced in "Almanac" is "The New Rule."

"Escape" is based on the painting *Young Hare* or *Wild Hare* in English by Albrecht Dürer, 1502.

The poems in "Quotidian: On Five Photographs by Deanna Dikeman" are based on her collection, *Relative Moments*, published by Chose Commune, 2024.

"On Viewing *Wing of a Blue Roller* by Albrecht Dürer" is based on the painting of the same name, 1512.

The title of *"Dreams of the Other Dreamers"* is from Walt Whitman's poem "The Sleepers."

The title of *"Does the Inertia of a Body Depend on Its Energy-Content?"* comes from the title of Albert Einstein's 1905 paper on relativity.

For "The Insomnia of Saint Symeon the Stylite," Saint Symeon (born c. 390 AD) spent thirty-seven years living on top of a pillar in Aleppo. Additionally, the italicized words are from Lord Alfred Tennyson's poem "St. Simeon Stylites."

Acknowledgments

Thank you to the following journals for publishing these poems, a few slightly revised:

Glass: Journal of Poetry: "Invention of the Helicopter"

The Classical Outlook: "Diana's Arrow," and republished in *A Folded History: Poems and Mythologies* and forthcoming in *Vox Populi Magazine*.

The Power of the Feminine: "Red Maples" and "Office Hours"

Flapper Poetry Café: "Sylvia Plath in the Night Realm," "For Allen Ginsberg's Mother," and "Heard on the Street."

Red Wheelbarrow: "Spring"

I-70 Review: "Bears," "The New Trees," originally titled "Cool Air Parts the Maples," "To Fold Like Marie Kondo," "Afloat," "The Insomnia of Saint Symeon the Stylite," "Escape," and "The Word *Samsara*" and "A Wind Named Sam"

Dunes Review: "Stolen" and "The Word Ache, with Its Own Sadness"

The Writer's Place Yearbook 2022, Vol 2: "Almanac," originally titled "Through the City, a Pandemic Journal"

The Shining Years: "Fat Tuesday at our Local Aldi"

Kansas Heartland: "Flowers in a Time of Plague"

Gratitude

My deep gratitude to Meadowlark Press for their efforts to bring this book into a reader's hands. My thanks to José Faus for selecting it as the 2025 Birdy Poetry Prize winner. I am grateful to many readers, writers, and artists for their generosity: Ruth Buchman, Susan Carman, Robert Cole, Maril Crabtree, Brian Daldorph, Pat Daneman, Deanna Dikeman, Cathryn Essinger, Rachel Hadas, Carolyn Hoppe, Beth Horning, Susanna Lang, Rebecca Hart Olander, Trish Reeves, Mary Silwance, Linda Tobaben, Barbara Varanka, and Maryfrances Wagner. Thanks also to Jan Weissmiller, owner of Prairie Lights Bookshop in Iowa City, Iowa, who led me to the newest edition of *The Collected Poems of Muriel Rukeyser* and the arc I could follow from that great poet's time to our own. Thank you to the poet-editors of *I-70 Review* for publishing many of these poems, and for nominating "Bears" for a Pushcart Prize.

About the Author

Catherine Anderson has published four collections of poetry, including *Everyone I Love Immortal* (Woodley Press, 2019), *Woman with a Gambling Mania* (Mayapple Press, 2014), *The Work of Hands* (Perugia Press, 2000), and *In the Mother Tongue* (Alice James Books, 1983). In 2022, a memoir about her late brother who had nonspeaking autism, *My Brother Speaks in Dreams: Of Family, Beauty & Belonging*, was published by Wising Up Press. She has been recognized for her poetry by the Massachusetts Artists' Foundation, the *Southern Humanities Review*, the *I-70 Review* and the *Crab Orchard Review*. Over the years, her poems have also appeared in the *Southern Review*, the *Harvard Review*, and the *Dunes Review*, among many others. She lives in Kansas City, where she has worked for over twenty years assisting new immigrants and refugees to become skilled interpreters. Learn more about Catherine at www.catherineanderson.uno

Meadowlark POETRY

Books are a way to explore, connect, and discover. Poetry invites us to observe and think in new ways, bridging our understanding of the world with our artistic need to interact with, shape, and share it with others.

Publishing poetry is our way of saying:
We love these words,
we want to preserve them,
we want to play a role in sharing them
with the world.

**Follow Meadowlark Press
on Facebook & Instagram**

(f) facebook.com/ReadAMeadowlarkBook

(O) @meadowlarkbooks

Birdy Poetry Prize Winners

2024
Warble
Alicia Rebecca Myers

I picked this collection because of how deeply the poet wrote from what Edward Hirsch calls "the poetry of affection," the poetry that connects us to our innate and vulnerable humanness. This quality is so vital when it comes to working with the fragments of brokenness, despair, and horror around us to craft a life, sustain a community, and behold the living earth with wonder and courage.
—Caryn Mirriam-Goldberg, *How Time Moves*

2023
Turkey Vulture
Zachary Lundgren

At first, the poems . . . seem like a portal to another place and time—a small town, a lifetime ago . . . Zachary Lundgren reminds us that there's no veil between the past and the present . . . In one sense, we aren't who we were in our youth. In another, we absolutely are. We are every version of ourselves we've ever been and ever will be.
—Melissa Fite Johnson, *Green*

2022
Cupping Our Palms
Jonathan Greenhause

These provocative, trustworthy poems owe their strength to narrators who are not afraid to confront their own sense of awe, misgivings, and incredulity, as it pertains to their various stations in life. The prevailing subject of parenthood, and what it means to shepherd children through the stages of growth, keeps circling in this superb collection.
—Bart Edelman, *Whistling to Trick the Wind*

2021
Knowing Is a Branching Trail
Alison Hicks

Knowing Is a Branching Trail captured my attention. I read in search of moments that create a soft pause in me. Time given back to me that allows me to sit with feeling, safely and freely. There were voices in the work that transitioned from stranger to companion. It felt as if we shared an understanding . . . I felt less alone with this book.

—Huascar Medina, *Un Mango Grows in Kansas*

2020
Selected Poems: 2000-2020
JC Mehta

With sharp and incisive language, each piece provides an immersive moment, inviting the reader into the experience of growing up half Cherokee, of self-harm and losing friends, of teaching and aging and loving and living in the Pacific Northwest. Nothing is veiled, nothing is alluded to, and their humor is ever-present, wry, and witty.

—Brenna Crotty, Editor, *Selected Poems*

2019
A Certain Kind of Forgiveness
Carol Kapaun Ratchenski

There is a worldliness in these poems, the kind of grit that accompanies a strong heart. There's awareness—of the self, of the world. And the poems are populated with the magical, husky things of this earth: warm beer in Berlin, rice in a bowl in a monastery, and stains from fresh cranberries. These are poems we can savor, now and again.

—Kevin Rabas, *More Than Words*

Meadowlark Press created The Birdy Poetry Prize to celebrate the voices of our era. Cash prize, publication, and 50 copies awarded annually.

Accepting Entries: September 1 - December 1

Entry Fee: $25

Prize: $1,000, publication by Meadowlark Press, 50 copies of the completed book

All entries will be considered for standard Meadowlark publishing contract offers, as well.

Full-length poetry manuscripts (55-page minimum) will be considered. Poems may be previously published in journals and/or anthologies but not in full-length, single-author volumes. Poets are eligible to enter, regardless of publishing history.

See meadowlarkbookstore.com for complete submission guidelines.

www.ingramcontent.com/pod-product-compliance
Lightning Source LLC
Chambersburg PA
CBHW020419130626
46549CB00006B/2639